Provided
by

Measure B

which was approved by
the voters in
November, 1998

Word Bird's

Winter Words

Published in the United States of America by The Child's World®, Inc.
PO Box 326
Chanhassen, MN 55317-0326
800-599-READ
www.childsworld.com

Project Manager Mary Berendes
Editor Katherine Stevenson, Ph.D.
Designer Ian Butterworth

Library of Congress Cataloging-in-Publication Data
Moncure, Jane Belk.
Word Bird's winter words / by Jane Belk Moncure.
p. cm.
Summary: Word Bird puts words about winter in his
word house—snow, mittens, sled, icicles, and others.
ISBN 1-56766-898-4 (lib. bdg.)
1. Vocabulary—Juvenile literature. 2. Winter—Juvenile literature.
[1. Vocabulary. 2. Winter. 3. Christmas.] I. Title.
PE1449 .M534 2001
428.1—dc21
00-010891

Word Bird's™

Winter Words

by Jane Belk Moncure

illustrated by Chris McEwan

Word Bird made a…

word house.

"I will put winter words
in my house," Word
Bird said.

Word Bird put in
these words:

snow

snowsuit

cap

scarf

mittens

boots

snowflakes

snowballs

snowman

snow shovels

sled

toboggan

snowshoes

skis

ice skates

fireplace

hot chocolate

icicles

holidays

Christmas

Hanukkah

Kwanzaa

New Year's Day

Can you read these winter

snow

boots

snowsuit

snowflakes

cap

snowballs

snowman

scarf

snow shovels

mittens

sled

words with Word Bird?

toboggan

 icicles

 snowshoes  holidays

skis  Christmas

 ice skates Hanukkah

fireplace  Kwanzaa

hot chocolate  New Year's Day

You can make a winter word house. You can put Word Bird's words in your house and read them, too.

cold

skis

Can you think of other winter words to put in your word house?